People Who Should Bring Out the Leader in You and Me

AFRICAN AMERICAN LEADERS FROM A-Z

Dr. ANDREA BERRY

Illustrated by Jasmine Mills

ABCDEF
GHIJKLM
NOPQRS
TUVWXYZ

To Andre and Anya who inspire me to be a better me.

~Dr. Andrea Berry~

Text Copyright ©2015

All rights reserved. No part of this publication may be reproduced, stored in a retrieval system of transmitted in any form by any means, electronic, mechanical, photocopying, or otherwise, without first obtaining written permission of the copyright owner.

Illustrations Copyright © 2015 Jasmine Mills
Edited and designed by TamikaInk.com
All Rights Reserved. Published in Maryland by
AB Publishing, Inc.
Greensboro, MD 21639

Publications. www.andreaberry.com

ISBN-13: 978-1507568552
LCCN: 2015904794
Printed in the U.S.A.

To Order Additional Copies:
Andrea Berry
andreaberryopher@gmail.com

A is for Althea Gibson who was an athlete with talent that went a long way.

Her accomplishments as a professional golfer and tennis player would make anyone say hip hip HORRAY!

B is for Bill Russell the basketball player whose skills made him a legend and role model for all. His Olympic wins and NBA honors grew to be like him... almost 7 feet tall.

C is for Charles Drew who gave time, energy and knowledge about medicine and matters of human blood plasma. His work is famously known from Wyoming to Alaska.

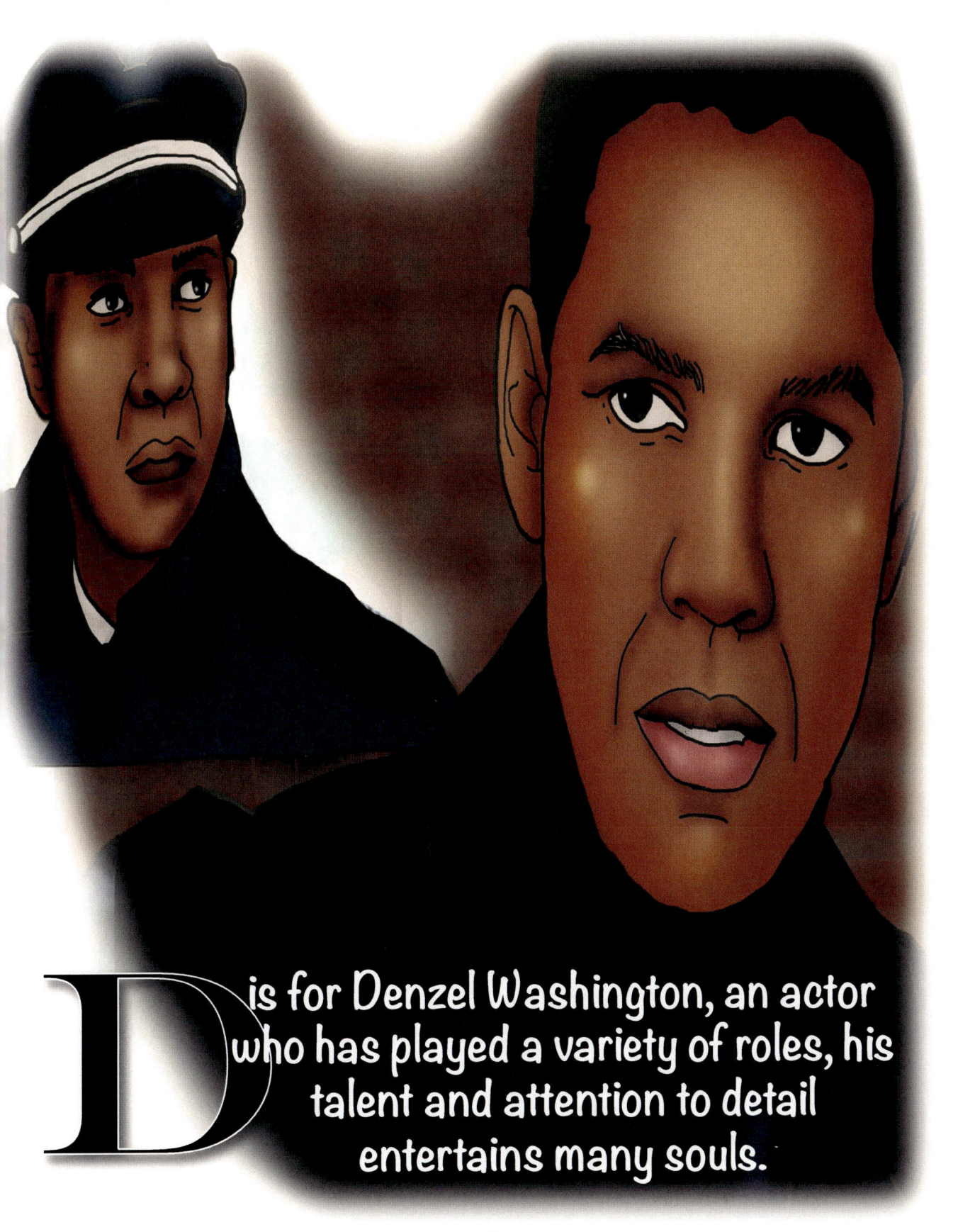

D is for Denzel Washington, an actor who has played a variety of roles, his talent and attention to detail entertains many souls.

E is for Ella Baker whose enthusiasm led to civil rights success.

Her life's work and mentoring make her one of history's best.

F is for Florence Griffith Joyner who was a track star who was fast and fancy: her beauty and talent made her an Olympic star. Her races attracted crowds from both near and far.

G is for Gwendolyn Brooks who was a poet with talent for miles. She published 75 poems by the age of 16 which generated lots of smiles.

H is for Herbie Hancock who is a music legend to many. His blends of jazz, classical and blues music have been admired by plenty.

I is for Ida B. Wells whose abilities to express herself in writing as a journalist were impressive. Her awards and accomplishments were certainly progressive.

J for is Jesse Owens whose track career showed lots of accomplishment and speed. Most of the national track records he would easily exceed.

K is for Kareem Abdul-Jabbar who was inducted into the basketball Hall of Fame. His excellent skills made him a famous athletic household name.

L is for LeBron James who is becoming a basketball legend at a very young age. One day in history he will have his very own page.

M is for Medger Evers who did civil rights work that helped us overcome segregation in the southern states. His drive gave us purpose and helped minimize racial hate.

N is for Nelly who is known for his rap songs. But, his other talents like songwriting, investing, and acting make his brand strong.

O is for Oprah Winfrey who has built a multi-million dollar media empire. As a result she succeeds at any project her heart desires.

P is for the pretty Phylicia Rashad, who is an actress who has won many awards. Since 1972 her career has been on a positive accord.

Q is for Queen Latifah who is a pioneer in her own right. From rapping to broadcasting and acting, her career is successful and continues to shine bright.

R is for Russell Simmons who is known as the third richest person in hip-hop. From music label, clothing lines and business, his money making potential does not stop.

S is for Spike Lee known as an icon in the film industry. This Emmy Award winner makes movies about difficult topics with dignity.

T is for Toni Morrison who is a professor, editor and novelist known for writing with lots of detail. Awards like the Nobel Peace Prize and the Presidential Medal of Freedom show she can do anything but fail.

U is for Ursala Burns who is the first black CEO of a Fortune 500 company and a woman making history. The title of 22nd most powerful woman in the world from FORBES tells quite a story.

V is for Vanessa Williams who may have endured a hard road at first. But, her success in modeling, singing, and acting shows a successful career reverse.

W is for Will Smith who is known by Newsweek as the most powerful actor in Hollywood. His career successes and awards have been much better than good.

X is for Malcolm X, who was a Muslim minister with lots of passion. He led a spiritual charge in a dignified and orderly fashion.

Y is for Yolanda Adams who graces people with her sweet gospel sound. She is by far one of the most classy gospel artists around.

Z is for Zora Neal Hurston who was an anthropologist and an author of short stories, novels and plays. She even wrote award winning essays.

ABCDEF
GHIJKLM
NOPQRS
TUVWXYZ

Made in the USA
Middletown, DE
15 May 2023